Stress Free
COLORING

new seasons®
a division of Publications International, Ltd.

Let's get social!

 @Publications_International

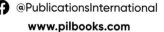 @PublicationsInternational

www.pilbooks.com

Living in harmony with nature's seasons awakens us to spring's renewal, fall's cozy slowness, winter's savory rest, and summer's exuberance. Thus we are reminded to honor each season's energies for the wisdom they hold.

Surround yourself with the serenity of nature, and you will feel more at peace with yourself and the world.

"In solitude we give passionate attention to our lives, to our memories, to the details around us."

—Virginia Woolf

"It is the sweet, simple things of life
which are the real ones after all."

—Laura Ingalls Wilder

I appreciate night, bright day's flip side.
I love its coolness—the dark velvet skies and
sparkling stars. If the sun burns hot, then
the moon is all cool beauty. The world
takes a breath. I am grateful for the
balance night brings.

"Rest is not idleness, and to lie sometimes on the grass under trees on a summer's day, listening to the murmur of the water, or watching the clouds float across the sky, is by no means a waste of time."

—Sir John Lubbock

In a busy life, I am grateful for those times when I can slow down. I am quiet and appreciative, and my heart is full.

"Our life is an apprenticeship to the truth that around every circle another can be drawn; that there is no end in nature, but every end is a beginning; that there is always another dawn risen on mid-noon, and under every deep a lower deep opens."

—Ralph Waldo Emerson

"Give me the splendid silent sun, with
all his beams full-dazzling".

–Walt Whitman

Never underestimate the power of a deep breath.

Many traditions consider birds to be winged spirits representing freedom, transcendence, and divinity. As for me, they just make me happy. I am grateful for the color and beauty of birds.

When your spirits are low, look up at the sky. Spot a bird soaring, a plane leaving contrails far above, maybe even a hot air balloon. These things that can conquer gravity can lift your heart as well.

Even the roughest thunderstorm is only temporary.

Good times teach you how to feel contentment.
Bad times teach you patience and faith. Joy
expands the heart and spirit. Struggles build
and resolve character. In all things, find grace.
At all times, be grateful.

Big achievements or joys do not happen every day, but if I am mindful, each day affords its small pleasures. Little things, so often overlooked, can contribute to deep satisfaction.

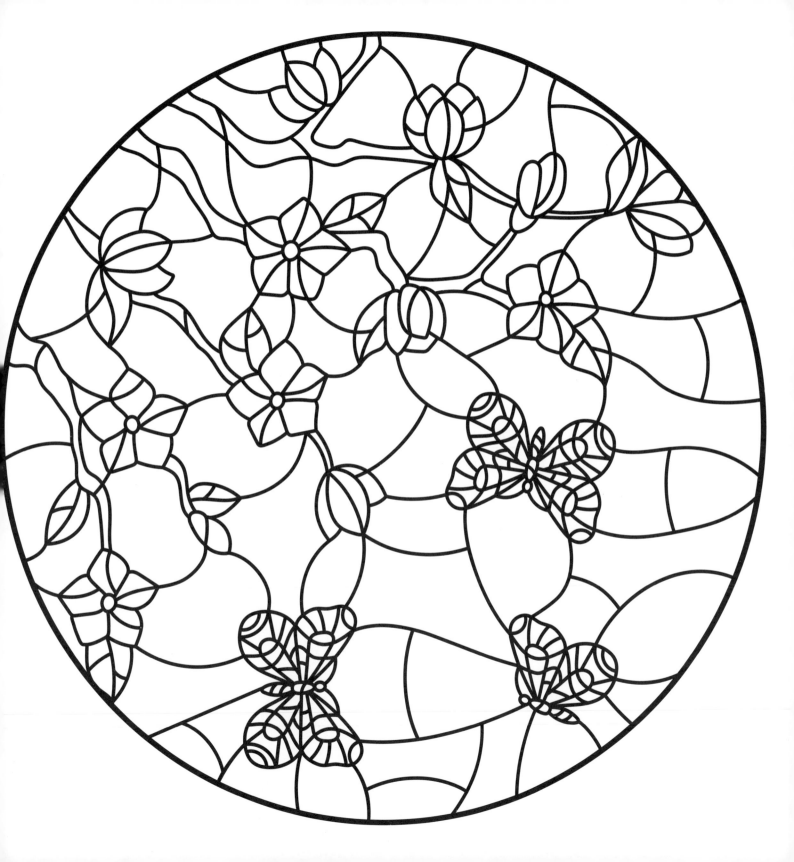

Balance is not always easy to achieve, and yet
I am joyful when I manage it. Time with loved
ones, time for meaningful work, time to be active,
time to be quiet, I am grateful for the days
when balance can be struck!

"Where there is great love, there are always miracles."

—Willa Cather

Happiness is a choice, and today I choose to be happy.

A calm spirit pours water on the hottest fire.

Gratitude removes blocks to happiness by keeping our focus in the here and now.

"What is the good of your stars and trees,
your sunrise and the wind, if they do
not enter into our daily lives?"

—E.M. Forster

Life's trials teach me patience and help me grow. I do not always like a challenge, but I am a better person for it!

"It is perhaps a more fortunate destiny to have a taste for collecting shells than to be born a millionaire."

—Robert Louis Stevenson

Give yourself permission to be happy every day.

Our most cherished moments are eternal.
We treasure them as they occur and savor them
over and over again as beloved memories.

"One small positive thought in the morning
can change your whole day."

Growing in wisdom means growing in love,
tolerance, grace, and acceptance.

The resilient heart withstands the winds of change, just as the flexible branch of a tree bends but does not break.

Those who choose to see the good in people will
be comforted by the goodness that abounds.

"Very early, I knew that the only object in life was to grow."
—Margaret Fuller

"The secret of happiness is not found in seeking
more, but in developing the capacity to enjoy less."

—Socrates

"Flowers are lovely; love is flower-like.
Friendship is a sheltering tree."

—Samuel Taylor Coleridge

Live with thanks for every experience life gives you.

On stormy days, stop and appreciate the clouds
scuttling across the sky, the smell of rain,
and the sudden crack of lightning.

Give thanks for warmth on cold days, for an hour spent in front of the fireplace with a good book, homemade quilts and afghans, and the taste of hot chocolate after a round of snow shoveling.

A pastime that involves silence and
little action can be a balm to the soul.

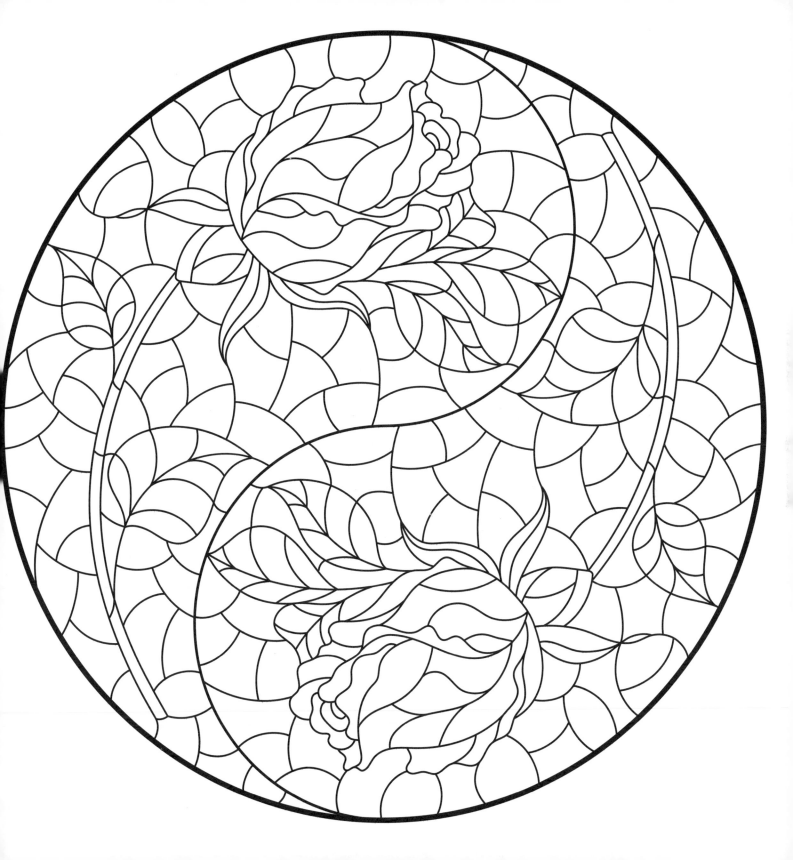

Change cultivates flexibility and open-mindedness; it is the catalyst for new experiences that help us flourish.

"Art washes away from the soul the dust of everyday life."

—Pablo Picasso

We start anew at each sunrise. What unique occurrence will happen today that may never happen again? What can we be thankful for this day, this hour, this moment?

From the moment we wake, our ears bring us the news. Coffee gurgles, birds sing. We like a new song on the radio. We communicate with and are warmed by the voices of those we love. Hearing connects us to the world and reminds us of its many blessings.

Good conversation can challenge and inspire.
It connects us to others, and helps us learn to
listen. Conversation helps us grow.

"The man is richest whose pleasures are cheapest."

—Henry David Thoreau

When we daydream, we look to the future and the past. Our creativity gets a jumpstart, and sometimes the solution to a seemingly unsolvable problem becomes clear. Honoring the time to reflect helps us stay aware of what's important to us. May we always make time to dip into ourselves and dream.

True wealth is inner peace.

There is no obstacle that you can't overcome.

Working in a garden can be a meditative
activity. It feels good to move the earth.
We weed and we plant; the air is fresh.
Gardens are good for the soul.

Solitude allows us the opportunity to
recharge—to just be—in a fast-paced world.

"Believe there is a great power silently
working all things for good, behave
yourself and never mind the rest."

—Beatrix Potter

All the flowers of all the tomorrows
are in the seeds of today.

"Ah! There is nothing like staying home for real comfort."

–Jane Austen

The more you open yourself up to
the goodness of the world, the more goodness
you will find the world has to give.

I am grateful for curiosity, which keeps
my brain elastic and my spirit young.

"The greatest weapon against stress is our
ability to choose one thought over another."

—William James

We lack for nothing when we are grateful for everything. That is when the blessings become a stream that never ceases to provide us with more to be grateful for.

The moon controls the tides and lights our way
in the darkness. Let us celebrate the mystery
of the moon's bright face!

"It is the appreciation of beauty and truth,
the striving for knowledge, which makes life worth living."

—Morris Raphael Cohen

Let us resist the tendency to take the shallow
route, and instead pursue depth in our lives.

"There are two ways of spreading light—to be the candle or the mirror that reflects it."

—Edith Wharton

"There's absolutely no reason for being rushed along with the rush. Everybody should be free to go very slow."

—Robert Frost

"Every act of love is a work of peace, no matter how small."

—Mother Teresa

"Tension is who you think you should be.
Relaxation is who you are."

—Chinese Proverb

The best things in life aren't things.

"The nearer a man comes to a calm mind the
closer he is to strength."

—Marcus Aurelius